Easy Gospel Songbook for Guitar

Book with Audio Access

By
Peter Vogl

For Free Online Audio Access
Go to this address on the internet:

http://cvls.com/extras/egsg

About This Book

This songbook features beginner to intermediate arrangements for classic hymns and gospel songs. These arrangements contain detailed strum patterns and chord progressions that are ideal for playing and singing along. The second portion of this book displays each song along with chord progressions, lyrics, and vocal melody lines. This is a great setup for sing-alongs because the lyrics are written in a large font so that multiple singers and musicians can read along.

Audio Tracks

This course also includes access to audio tracks to help you learn and practice. We have included three different recordings of each song. The first version features the guitar playing along with other instruments. The second recording features the other instruments with no guitar so that you can practice playing the guitar part in context. The third version is the guitar by itself. You may access these files by going to the following web address:

http://cvls.com/extras/egsg

The Author

Peter started playing guitar in 2nd grade and very quickly realized his calling. He played in several bands through his years at Okemos High, and proceeded to study classical guitar in college at the University of Georgia under the tutelage of John Sutherland. After receiving his undergraduate degree in Classical Guitar Performance Peter continued with his studies on a assistantship at James Madison University.

Peter moved back to Georgia and began playing the club circuit in Atlanta as a soloist and with a multitude of bands. He also founded and managed several schools of guitar including the Guitar Learning Center. During this time Peter produced many products for Watch & Learn Inc. such as *The Guitarist's Chord Book, The Guitarist's Scale Book, Intro to Blues Guitar, Intro to Rock Guitar, The Guitarist's Tablature Book, & The Let's Jam! Series.*

In the 90's Peter met Jan Smith and began to play with the Jan Smith Band performing on several of her CDs including Nonstop Thrill, Surrender, and Resurrection. In 2001 Peter moved into Jan Smith Studios where he continues to teach and do session work with local and national talent. Peter has performed on stage with talents such as Michael Bolton, Cee-Lo, Kelly Price, Steve Vai, Earl Klugh, Sharon Isbon, and Sleepy Brown. In collaboration with the NARAS organization he is the band leader each year at the Heroes Award Dinner in Atlanta.

More Guitar Books

   To brush up on your technique, try the *Acoustic Guitar Deluxe Edition with Online Video & Audio.* This beginner course teaches playing position, strumming, chords, and how to read guitar tabs. Includes a complete chord chart, an hour of video instruction, and all music is written in both standard music notation and tablature with lyrics and melody lines. Contains 18 songs demonstrated at three speeds along with an acoustic band, including vocals

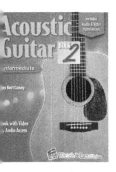

   The follow-up course, *Acoustic Guitar Book 2 with Online Video & Audio,* takes you to the next level of playing rhythm guitar by teaching a variety of rock & country strums, arpeggios, bar chords, and how to play along with other guitarists. The student plays and sings along with a full band on extended versions of 17 popular songs.

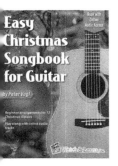

   The *Christmas Songbook for Guitar* with Online Audio Access features beginner to intermediate arrangements for classic Christmas songs. Each song features detailed strum patterns, chord charts, lyrics, and vocal melody notation. Section 2 displays each song with extended lyrics and chord progressions. This is a great for sing-alongs because the lyrics are written in a large font so that multiple singers and musicians can read along. This course also includes online access to audio tracks to help you learn and practice.

   The *Bluegrass Fakebook* contains lyrics, chord progressions, and melody lines to 150 of the all-time favorite Bluegrass songs, including 50 gospel tunes as well as many "new" bluegrass songs. Printed in large, easy-to-read type with one song per page, this book is excellent for use on stage or in jam sessions, because everyone can read along. Also includes chord charts for the guitar, banjo, and mandolin.

  These products are available on Amazon.com. If you have any questions, problems, or comments, please contact us at:

Watch & Learn, Inc.
2947 East Point St.
East Point, GA 30344
800-416-7088
sales@cvls.com

Table of Contents

Section 3 - Lyrics

Tuning the Guitar

Before playing the guitar, it must be tuned to standard pitch. If you have a piano at home, it can be used as a tuning source. The following picture shows how to tune the guitar to the piano.

Note: If your piano hasn't been tuned recently, the guitar may not agree perfectly with a pitch pipe or tuning fork. Some older pianos are tuned a half step below standard pitch. In this case, use one of the following methods to tune.

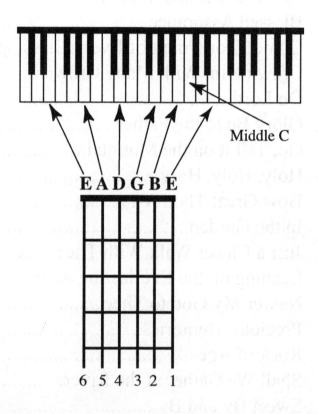

Middle C

E A D G B E

6 5 4 3 2 1

ELECTRONIC TUNER

An electronic tuner is the fastest and most accurate way to tune a guitar. I highly recommend getting one. It may take months or years for a beginner to develop the skills to tune a guitar correctly by ear. The electronic tuner is more precise and used by virtually every professional guitar player.

TIP *Never leave your instrument in a car or trunk during extreme heat or cold.*

Guitar Notation

The guitar notation in this book is written on two lines or staves. The top staff is the melody line with lyrics. The bottom line is the strumming pattern for the right hand.

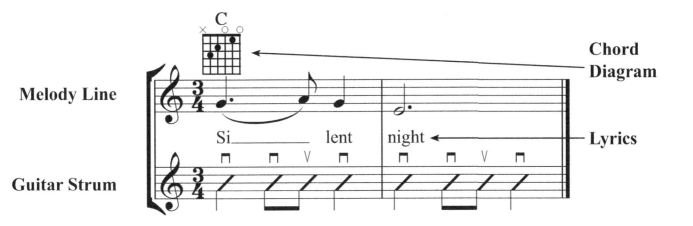

The exercises contain only one line or staff. This is the guitar strumming notation.

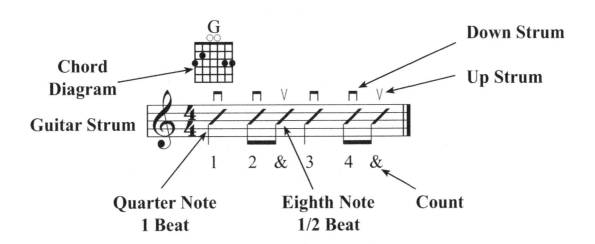

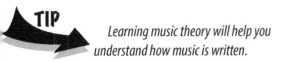 *Learning music theory will help you understand how music is written.*

Section 2
The Songs

Online Audio Access is available at this address on the internet:

http://cvls.com/extras/egsg

Chord Diagrams

The first song is a five chord song in the key of G and we'll use the G, C, D, A, and Am chords.

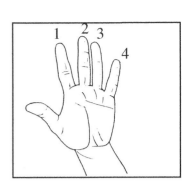

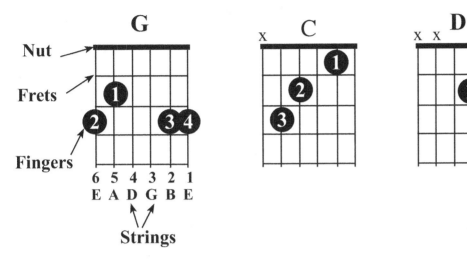

Strum Pattern

This song is in 3/4 time which means there are three beats per measure and we count 1 2 3 , 1 2 3. The strum pattern will be down down up down and is counted:

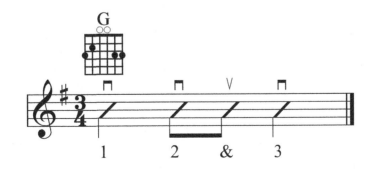

Blessed Assurance

Chord Diagrams

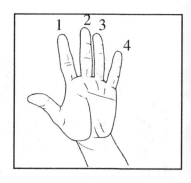

The next song is a four chord song in the key of G and we'll use the C, G, and D, and Em chords.

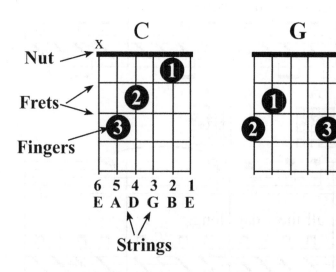

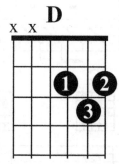

Strum Exercise

Amazing Grace is in 3/4 time, which means there are 3 beats per measure and we count 1 2 3, 1 2 3. The strum will be down down down up and is counted:

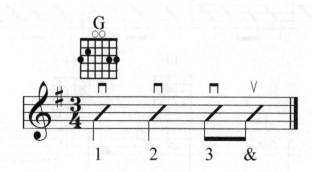

12

Amazing Grace

Chords

Rock of Ages is in the key of C and we'll use the F, C, & G chords.

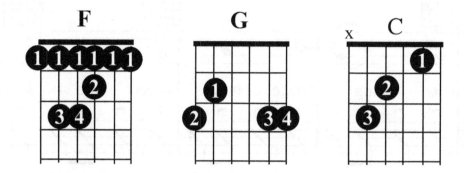

Strum Pattern

This song is in 3/4 time which means there are three beats per measure and we count 1 2 3 , 1 2 3. The strum pattern will be down down down up and is counted:

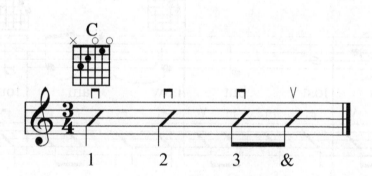

Rock of Ages

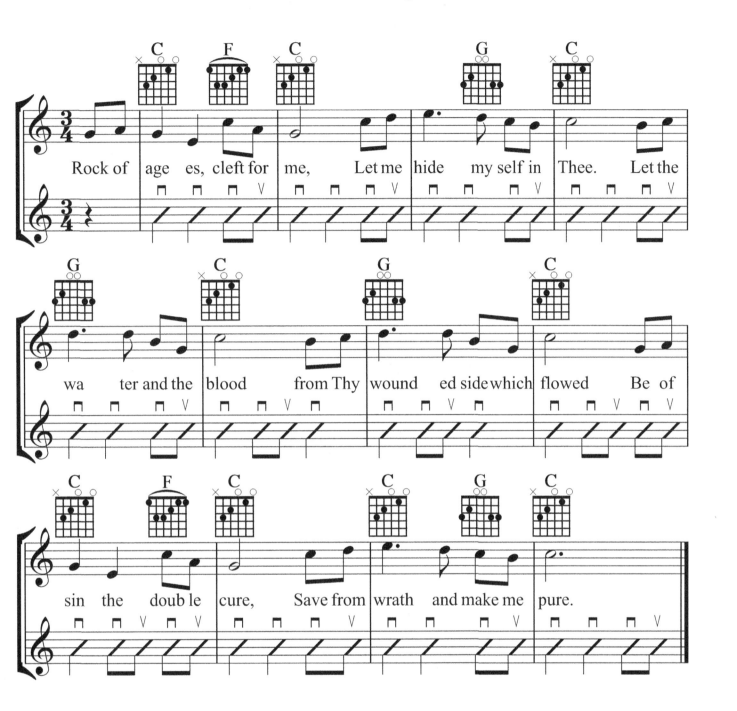

Chords

Six chords in the next song, adding Bm and C#dim⁷ to the four we've already used.

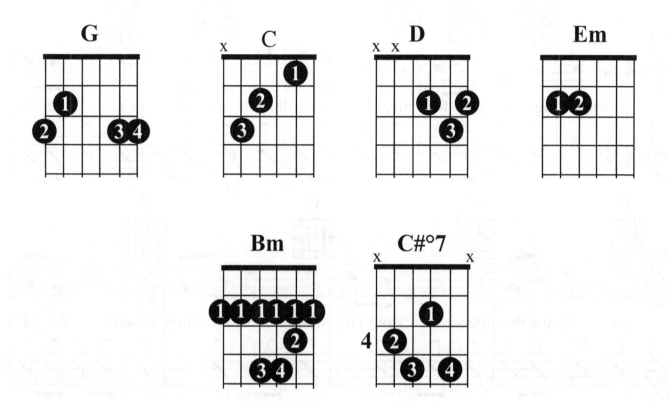

Strum Pattern

This song is in 4/4 time and the strum will be down down down down up and is counted 1 2 3 4 &.

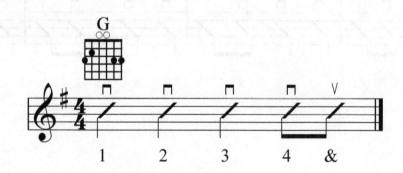

Nearer My God to Thee

Chords

Let's add the Dm to our repertoire.

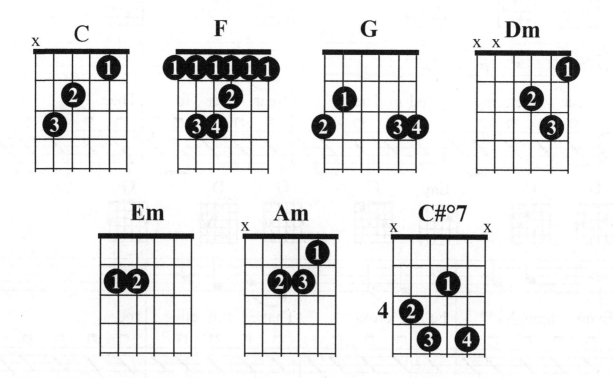

Strum Pattern

This song is in 4/4 time and the strum will be down down up down down up and is counted:

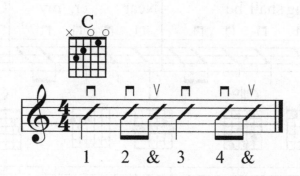

Shall We Gather at the River

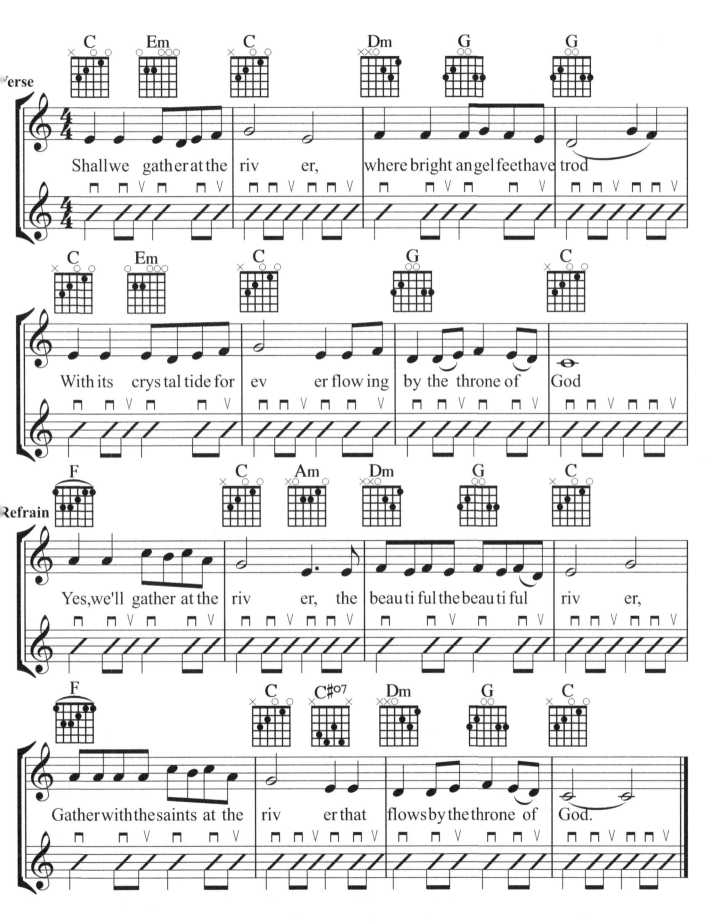

Chords

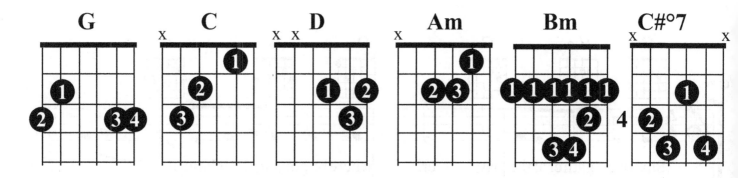

Strum Pattern

The strum for this pattern is down down up down down up.

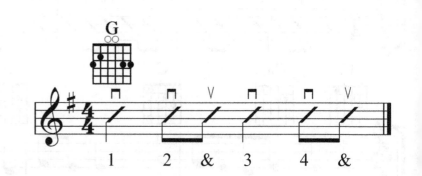

Sweet By and By

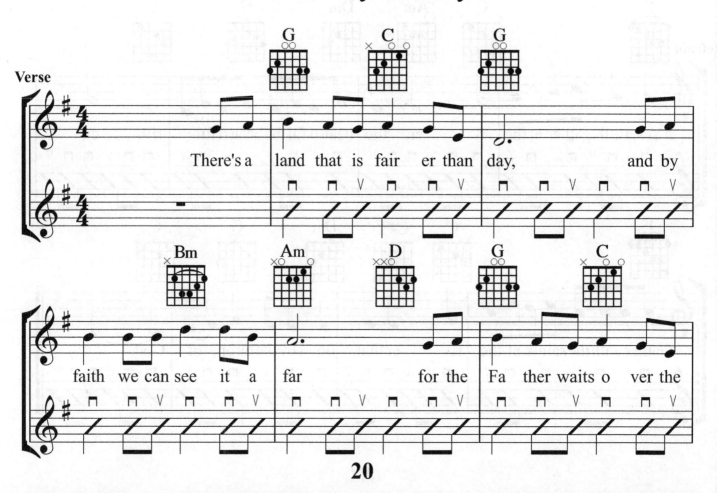

Verse

There's a | land that is fair er than day, | and by
faith we can see it a | far | for the | Fa ther waits o ver the

Refrain

21

Chords

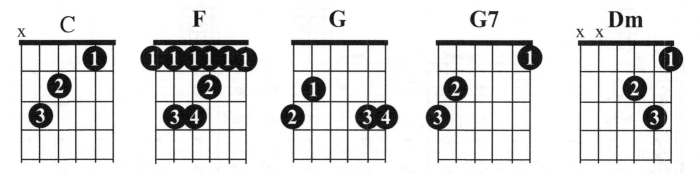

Strum Pattern

This song is in 3/4 time and the strum will be down down up down down up and is counted:

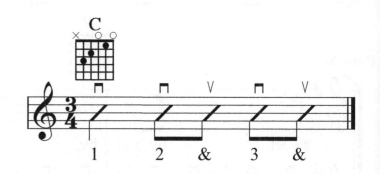

The Old Rugged Cross

Chords

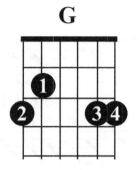 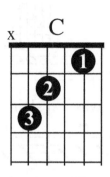 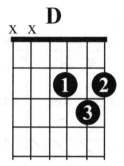 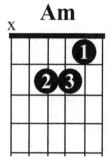

Strum Pattern

This song is in 4/4 time and the strum will be down down down up down up and is counted:

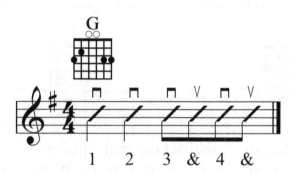

What a Friend We Have in Jesus

24

Chords

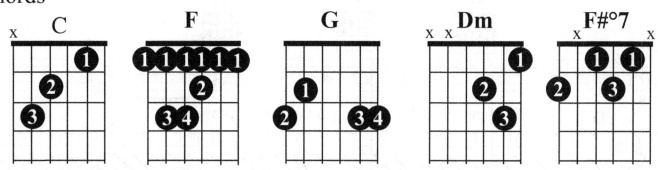

Strum Pattern

This song is in 4/4 time and the strum will be down down down down up and is counted:

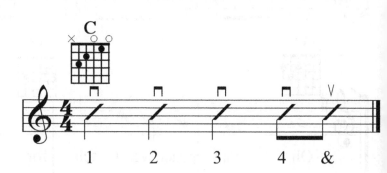

How Great Thou Art

Verse

O Lord my God,   when I in awe some won der   con sid er

all   the worlds Thy hands have made.   I see the stars,   I hear the rolling

26

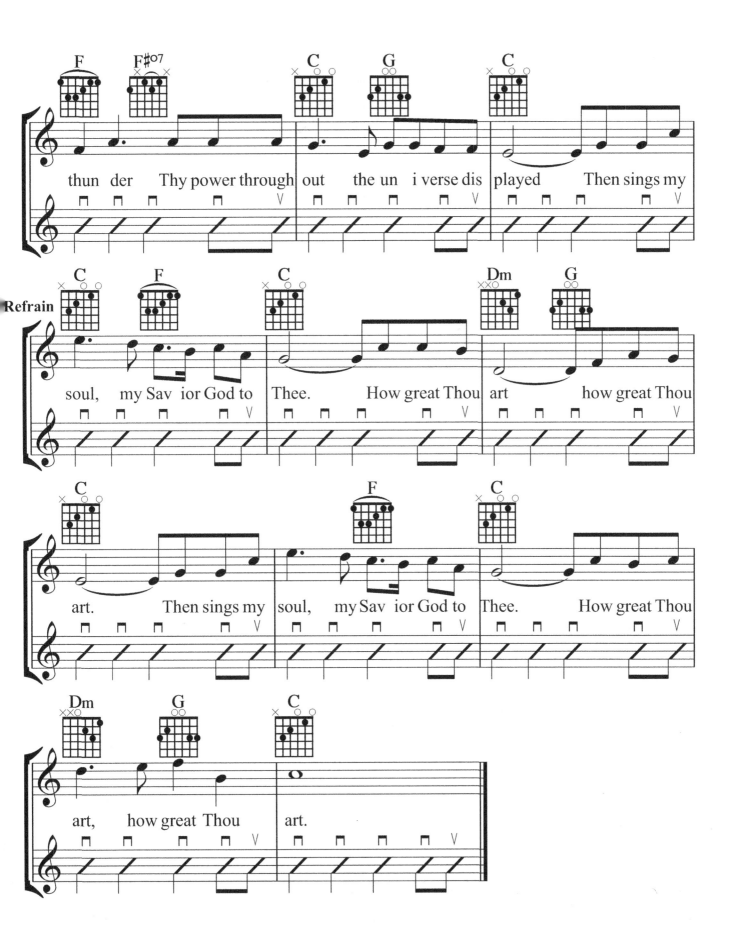

27

Chords

B⁷ is the new chord in this song.

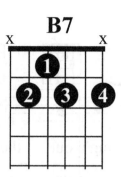

Strum Pattern

This song is in 3/4 time and the strum will be bass down down. The bass note will be the root note of the chord, so G for G chord, C for C chord, etc.

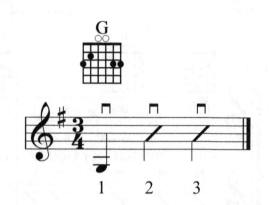

In The Garden

Verse

I come to the gar den a lone   while the dew is

still on the ros   es   and the voice I hear fall ing on my

Refrain

29

Chords

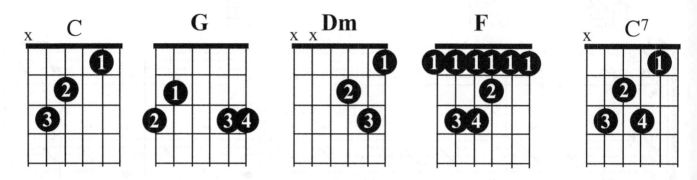

Strum Pattern

This song is in 4/4 time and the strum will be down down down down up and is counted:

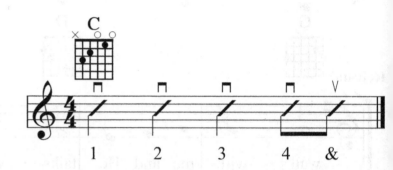

Just a Closer Walk with Thee

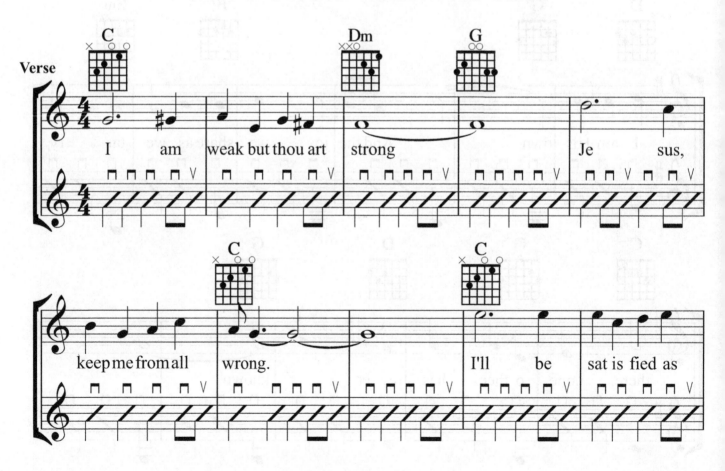

30

Chords

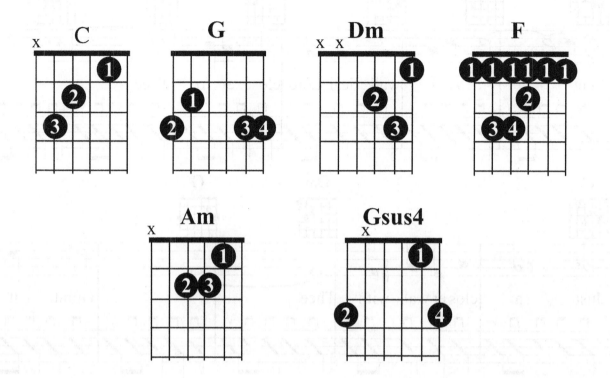

Strum Pattern

This song is in 4/4 time and the strum will be down down up down down up and is counted:

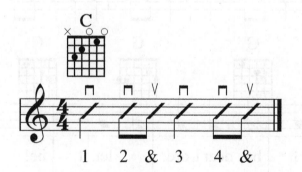

Leaning on the Everlasting Arms

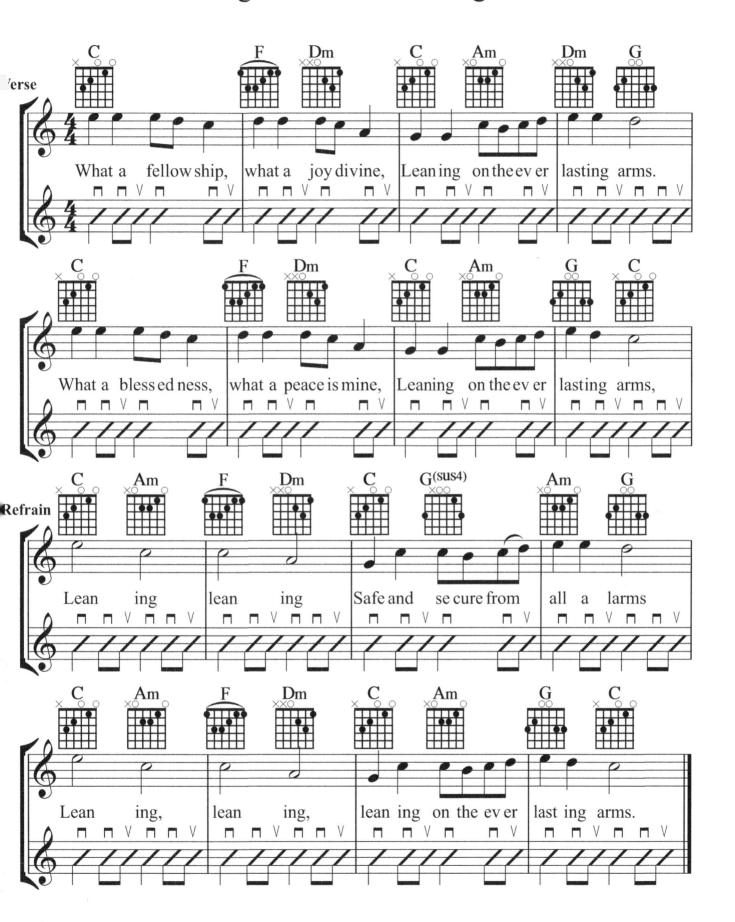

Chords

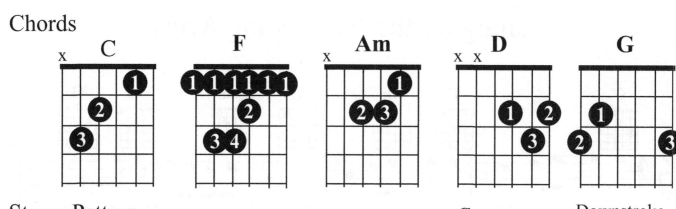

Strum Pattern

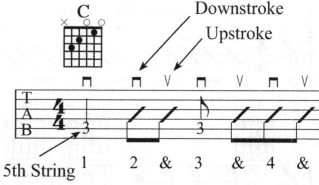

The next five songs use bass notes with the strum. We'll use guitar tablature for these songs. Each of the six lines represent a string on the guitar with the lowest line being the 6th string or lowest note. We'll play bass notes on the 6th string, 5th string, and 4th string. This song is in 4/4 time which means it has 4 beats to a measure. For the C chord, play a bass note on the 5th string and then a strum pattern. The bass note is the root note of each chord (C note for C chord, G note for G chord, etc). The strum pattern is counted 1 2 & 3 & 4 &, bass down up bass up down up.

Precious Memories

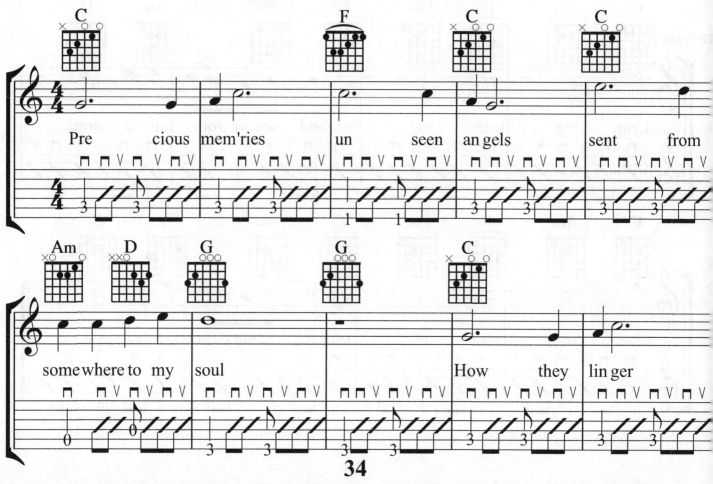

Chords

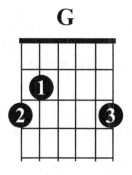
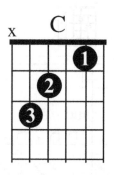
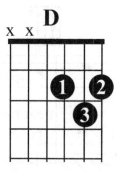

Strum Pattern

This song is in 4/4 time and has one strum played throughout.

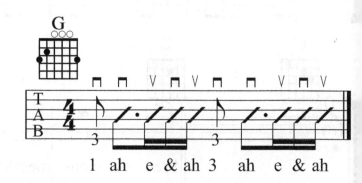

1 ah e & ah 3 ah e & ah

Uncloudy Day

O they tell me of a home far be yond the skies, O they tell me of a home far a way O they tell me of a home where no

37

Chords

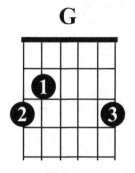 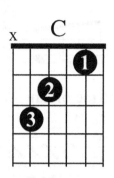 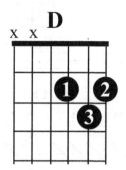 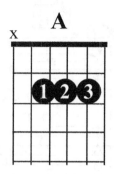

Strum Pattern

This song is in 4/4 time. It utilizes a bass note strum pattern. Pay attention to the bass notes.

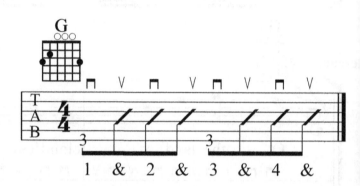

When the Roll is Called Up Yonder

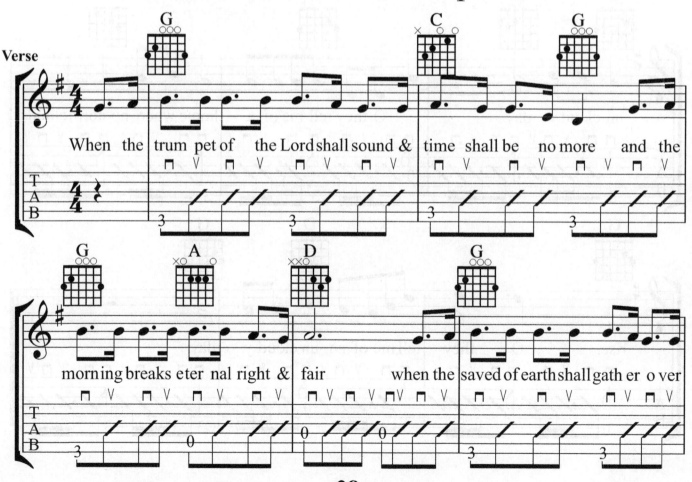

38

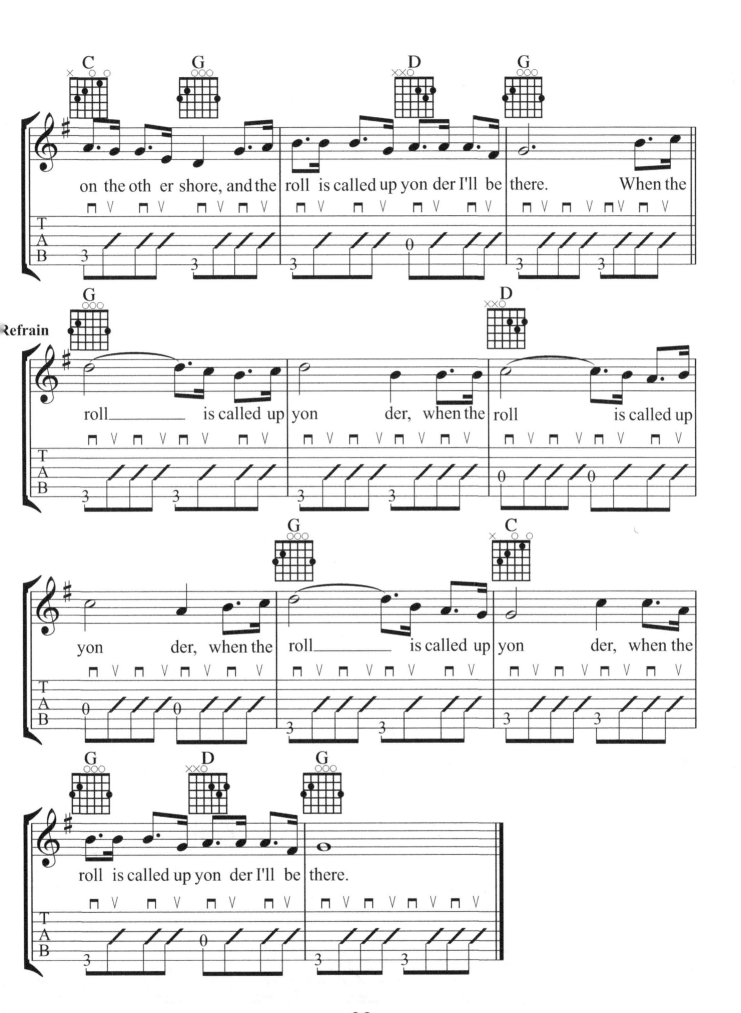

39

Chords

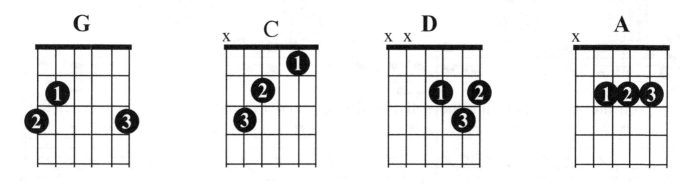

Strum Pattern

This song is in 4/4 time and uses a couple of different patterns. Pay attention to the bass notes.

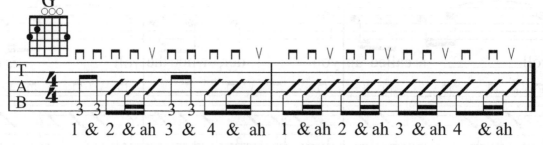

1 & 2 & ah 3 & 4 & ah   1 & ah 2 & ah 3 & ah 4 & ah

Are You Washed in the Blood

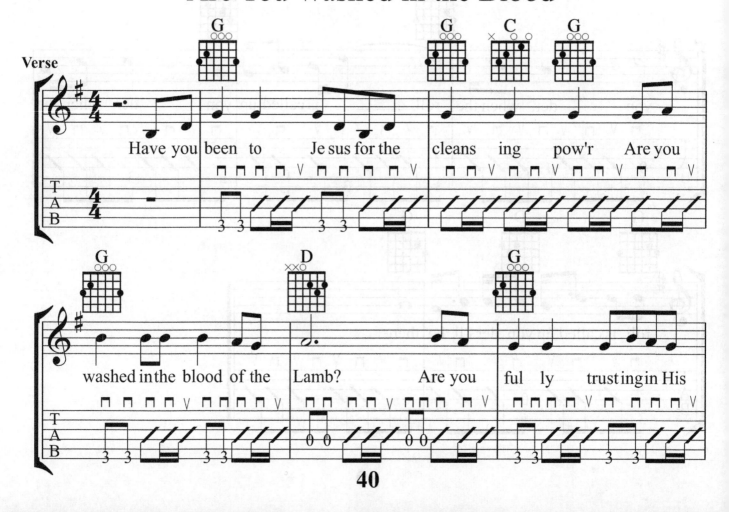

Verse

Have you been to   Je sus for the   cleans ing   pow'r   Are you

washed in the blood of the   Lamb?   Are you   ful ly   trust ing in His

40

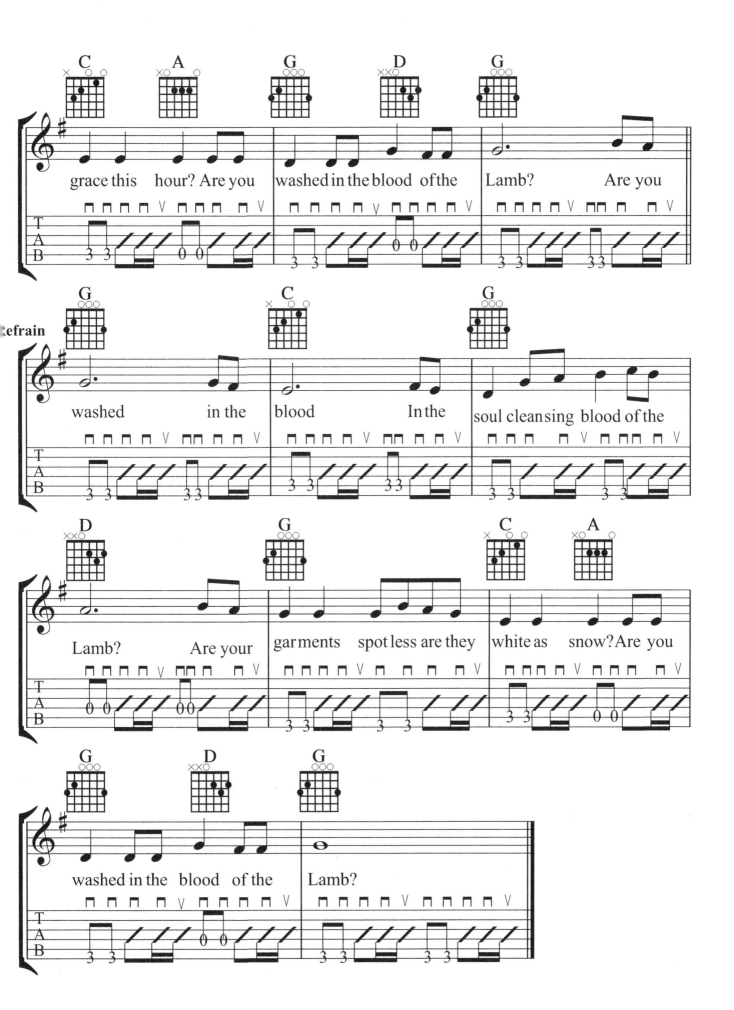

41

Chords

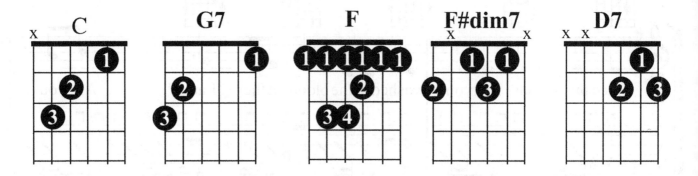

Strum Pattern

This song is in 4/4 time and has a couple of strum patterns. Pay attention to the bass notes.

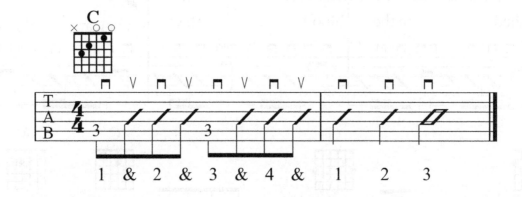

When We All Get to Heaven

Verse

Sing the won drous love of__ Je sus, sing His mer_ cy__

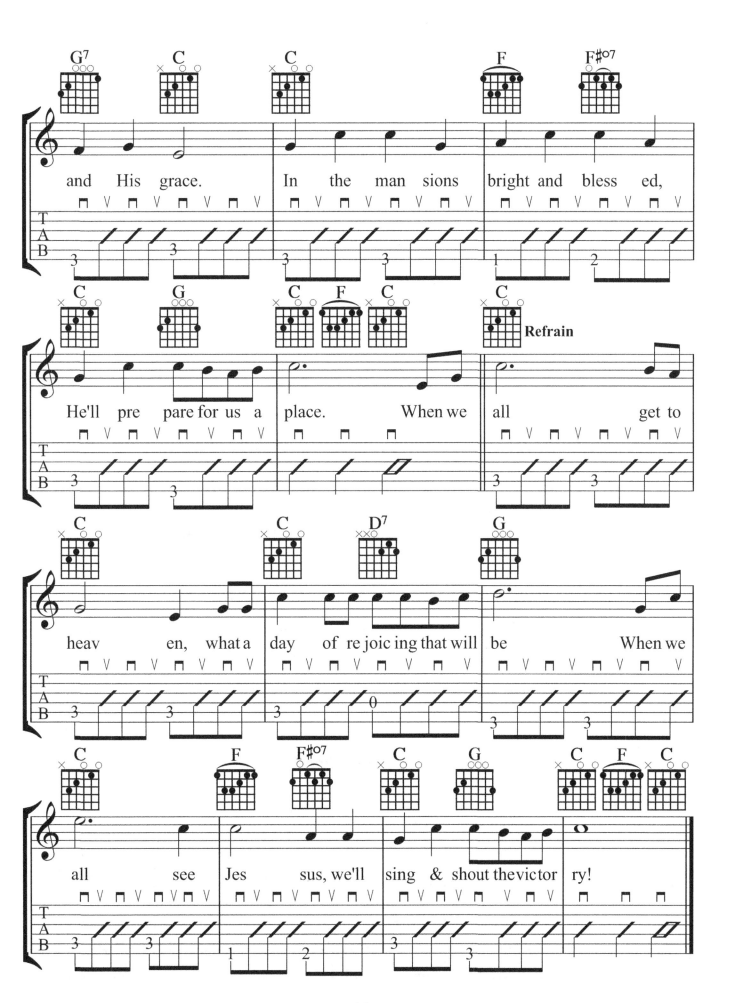

43

Chords

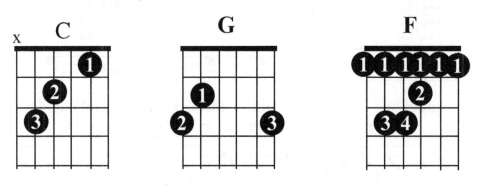

Strum Pattern

The next seven songs don't use a bass note, so we'll use standard guitar notation which has five lines. This song is in 3/4 time and has a repeating strum pattern throughout.

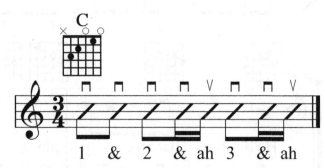

Come Thou Fount of Every Blessing

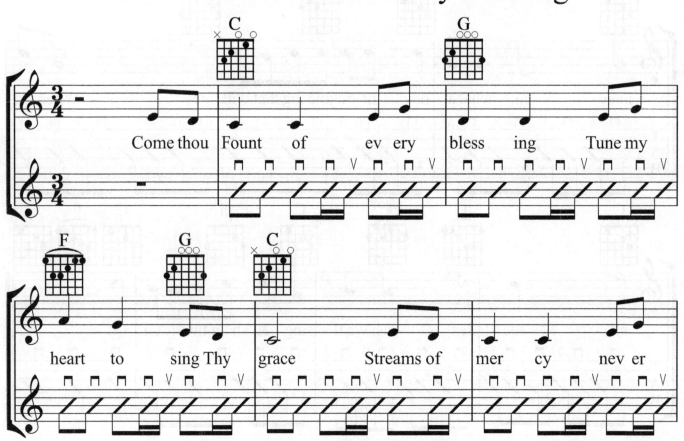

Come thou Fount of ev ery bless ing Tune my
heart to sing Thy grace Streams of mer cy nev er

Chords

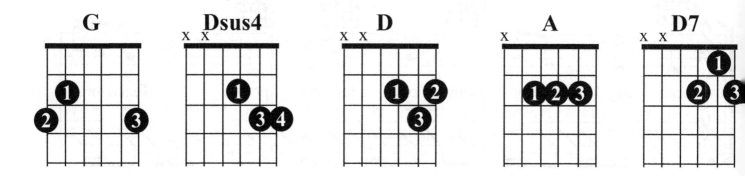

Strum Pattern

This song is in 4/4 time and has a couple different strum patterns.

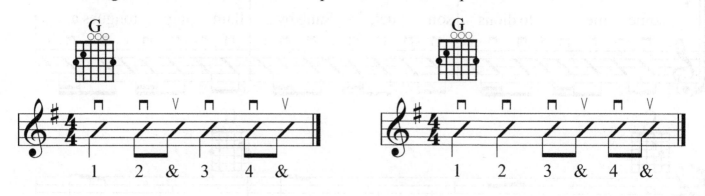

Glory Be to the Father

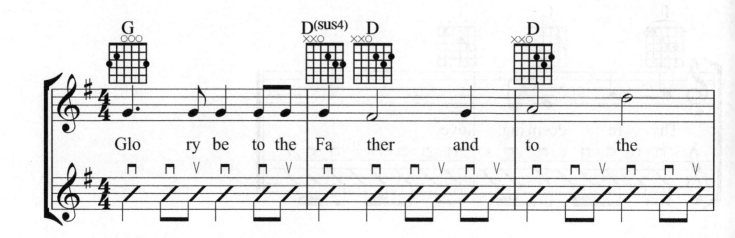

Glo ry be to the Fa ther and to the

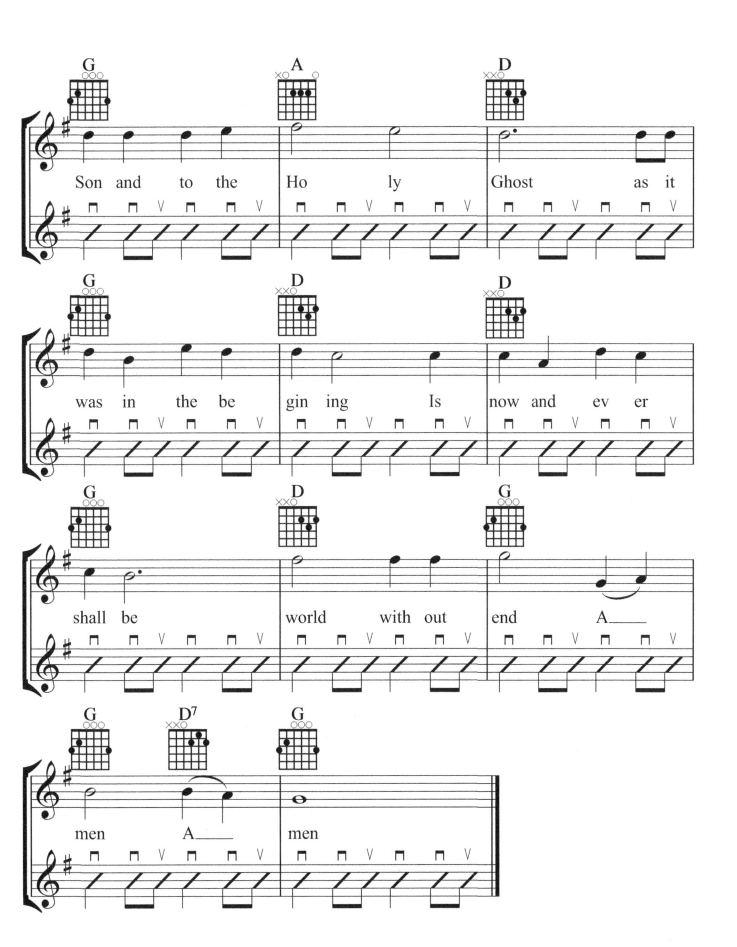

G A D
Son and to the Ho ly Ghost as it
G D D
was in the be gin ing Is now and ev er
G D G
shall be world with out end A
G D7 G
men A men

Chords

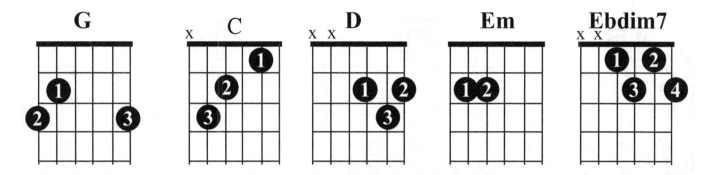

Strum Pattern

This song is in 4/4 time and uses a couple of different strum patterns.

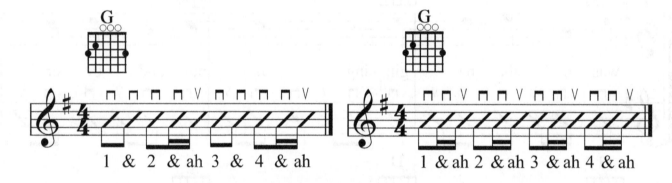

1 & 2 & ah 3 & 4 & ah

1 & ah 2 & ah 3 & ah 4 & ah

Do Lord

Verse

I've got a home in glo ry land that out shines the sun,

I've got a home in glo ry land that out shines the sun,

48

49

Chords

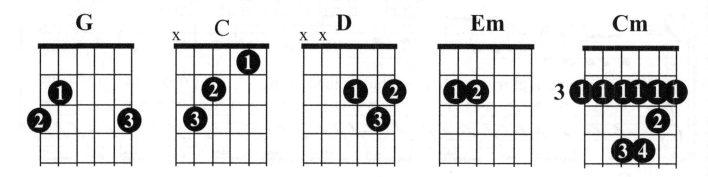

Strum Pattern

This song is in 4/4 time and has a very basic strum pattern. Pay attention to the accents.

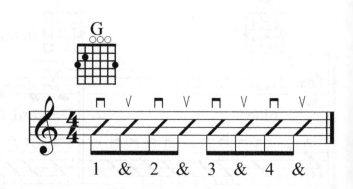

Swing Low Sweet Chariot

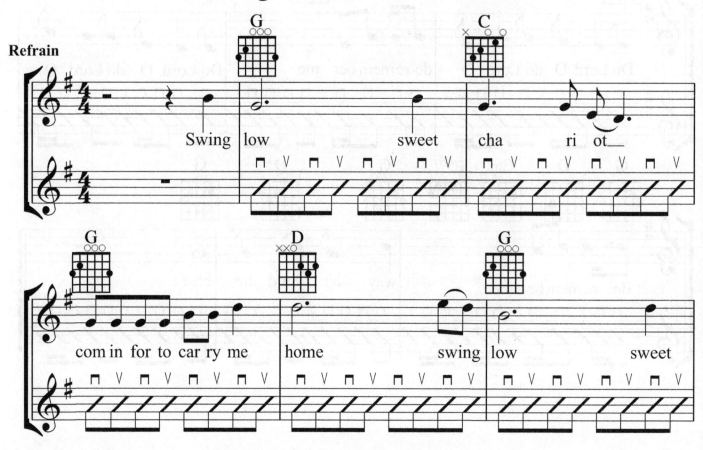

50

Chords

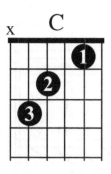
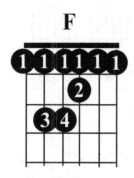
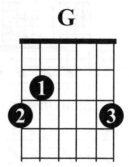
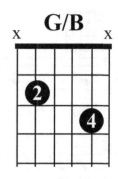

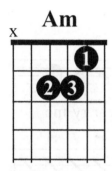
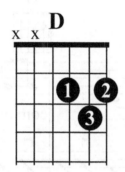

Strum Patterns

This song is in 4/4. It has a couple of different strum patterns.

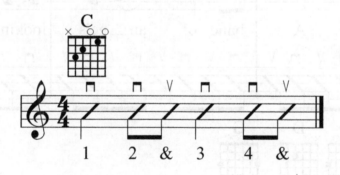

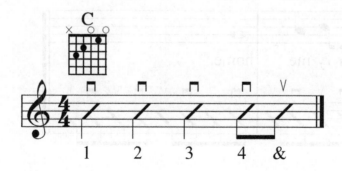

Holy, Holy, Holy

Chords

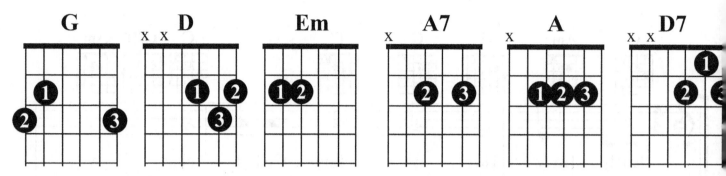

Strum Pattern

This song is in 4/4 time and has one strum pattern.

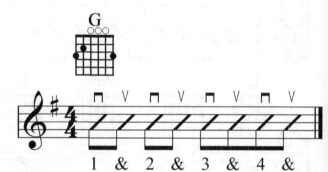

1 & 2 & 3 & 4 &

Go Tell it on the Mountain

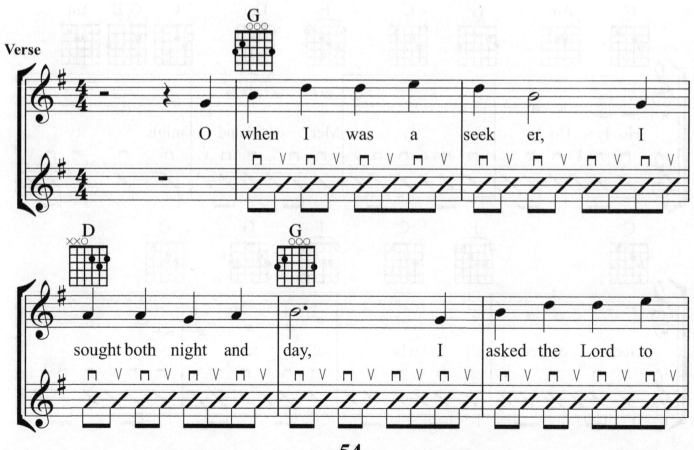

55

Crown Him With Many Crowns
Chords & Strums

Chords

There are six chords in this song with a couple of new ones.

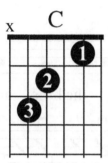
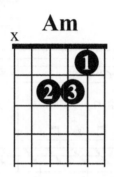
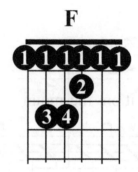
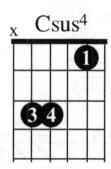

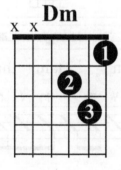

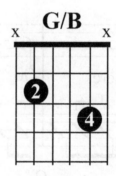
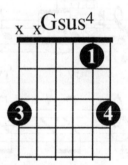

Strum Patterns

This song is in 4/4 time and has three very similar strum patterns.

Strum Pattern 1

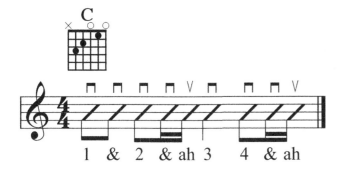

Strum Pattern 2

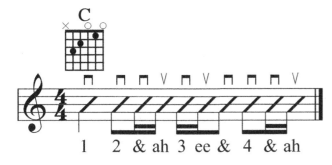

Strum Pattern 3

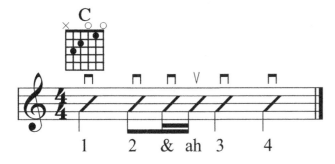

Crown Him With Many Crowns

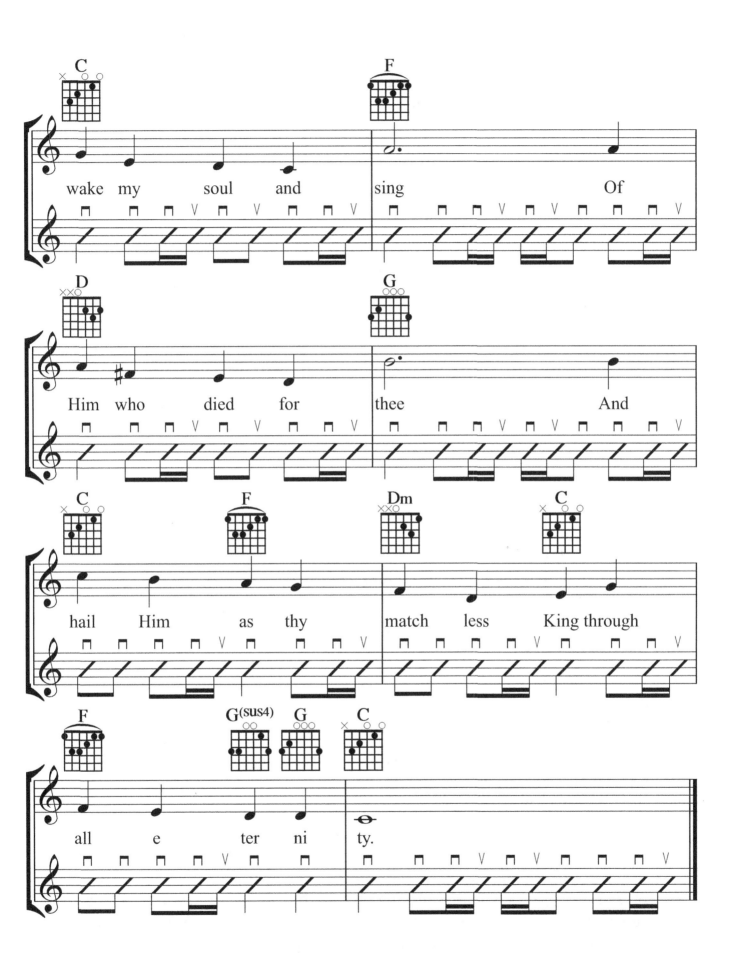

Lyrics

This section contains the melody line, lyrics, and chord progressions so that you can play the complete version of the songs with all of the lyrics. This also works great for jam sessions or playing on stage because the lyrics are in a large font with the chord progression on each verse. This section is also arranged in alphabetical order to make finding the songs easier.

Amazing Grace

A   maz   ing   Grace   how   sweet   the

sound,   that   saved   a   wretch   like   me.

I   once   was   lost   but   now   am

found.   Was   blind   but   now   I   see

'Twas grace that taught my heart to fear
And grace my fears relieved.
How precious did that grace appear
The hour I first believed

Through many dangers, toils, and snares,
I have already come.
Tis grace has brought me safe this far,
And grace will lead me home.

When we've been here ten thousand years
Bright shining as the sun
We've no less days to sing God's praise
Than when we first begun

Are You Washed in the Blood

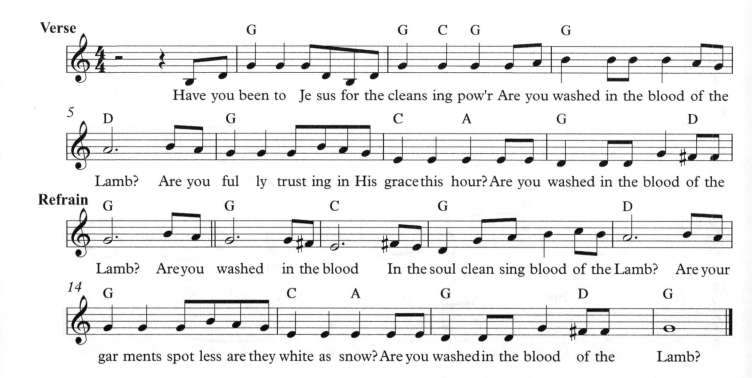

Verse

Have you been to Je sus for the cleans ing pow'r Are you washed in the blood of the Lamb? Are you ful ly trust ing in His grace this hour? Are you washed in the blood of the

Refrain

Lamb? Are you washed in the blood In the soul clean sing blood of the Lamb? Are your gar ments spot less are they white as snow? Are you washed in the blood of the Lamb?

Are you walking daily by the Savior's side
^G   ^C ^{G.}
Are you washed in the blood of the Lamb
^G   ^D
Do you rest each moment in the Crucified
^G   ^C ^A
Are you washed in the blood of the Lamb
^G   ^D   ^G
Refrain

When the Bridegroom cometh will your robes be white
^{G.}   ^C ^G
Are you washed in the blood of the Lamb
^G   ^D
Will your soul be ready for the mansions bright
^G   ^C ^{A.}
And be washed in the blood of the Lamb
^G   ^D   ^G
Refrain

Lay aside the garments that are stained with sin
^{G.}   ^C   ^{G.}
And be washed in the blood of the Lamb
^G   ^D
There's a fountain blowing for the soul unclean
^G   ^C ^A
O be washed in the blood of the Lamb
^G   ^D   ^G
Refrain

62

Blessed Assurance

Verse

Bless ed as sur ance, Je sus is mine! Oh, what a fore taste of glor y di vine! Heir of sal va tion, pur chase of God, Born of His Spir it washed in His blood.

Refrain

This is my sto ry, this is my song. Prais ing my Sav ior, all the day long. This is my sto ry, this is my song Prais ing my Sav ior all the day long

Perfect submission, perfect delight.
Visions of rapture now burst on my sight.
Angels descending bring from above
Echoes of mercy, whispers of love
Refrain

Perfect submission, all is at rest.
I in my Savior am happy and blessed.
Watching and waiting looking above.
Filled with His goodness, lost in His love.
Refrain

Come Thou Fount of Every Blessing

Come, thou Fount of every blessing, Tune my heart to sing Thy grace Streams of mercy never ceasing Call for songs of loudest praise. Teach me some melodious sonnet, Sung by flaming tongues above: Praise the mount, I'm fixed upon it, Mount of Thy redeeming love.

Here I raise mine Ebenezer, hither by Thy help I'm come
And I hope, by Thy good pleasure, safely to arrive at home
Jesus sought me when a stranger, wand'ring from the fold of God
He to rescue me from danger, interposed His precious blood

Oh, that day when freed from sinning, I shall see Thy lovely face
Clothed then in the blood washed linen, how I'll sing Thy wondrous grace
Come, my Lord, no longer tarry, take my ransomed soul away
Send Thine angels now to carry me to realms of endless day

O to grace how great a debtor daily I'm constrained to be
Let Thy goodness, like a fetter, bind my wand'ring heart to Thee
Prone to wander, Lord, I feel it, prone to leave the God I love
Here's my heart, O take and seal it, seal it for Thy courts above

Crown Him With Many Crowns

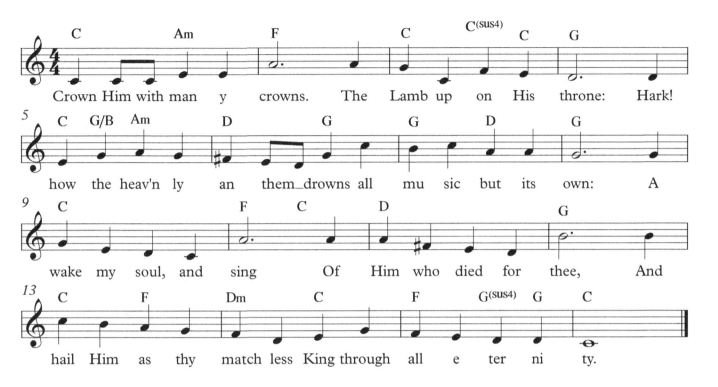

Crown Him with man y crowns. The Lamb up on His throne: Hark!

how the heav'n ly an them drowns all mu sic but its own: A

wake my soul, and sing Of Him who died for thee, And

hail Him as thy match less King through all e ter ni ty.

     C   Am   F   C   Csus⁴   C G
Crown Him the Son of God, Before the worlds began
     C   G/B Am   D   G   D   G
And ye, who tread where He hath trod, crown Him the Son of Man
     C   F   C   D   G
Who every grief hath known that wrings the human breast
     C   F   Dm   C   F Gsus⁴ G C
And takes and bears them for His own, That all in Him may rest

     C   Am   F   C   Csus⁴ C G
Crown Him the Lord of life, Who triumphed o'er the grave,
     C   G/B Am   D   G   D   G
Who rose victorious in the strife for those He came to save
     C   F   C   D   G
His glories now we sing Who died, and rose on high
     C   F   Dm   C   F Gsus⁴ G   C
Who died, Eternal life to bring, And lives that death may die

     C   Am   F   C   Csus⁴   C G
Crown Him the Lord of heav'n, Enthroned in worlds above
            C G/B Am   D   G   D   G
Crown Him the king, to whom is given, the wondrous name of Love
     C   F   C   D   G
Crown Him with many crowns, As thrones before Him fall,
     C   F   Dm   C   F Gsus⁴ G C
Crown Him, ye kings with many crowns, He is King of all

Do Lord

I took Jesus as my Savior you take Him too
I took Jesus as my Savior you take Him too
I took Jesus as my Savior you take Him too
While He's calling you

Refrain

Peter will be waiting with a welcome just for me
Angels songs will fill the air through all eternity
That will be a joyful everlasting jubilee
Far away beyond the blue

Refrain

Glory Be to the Father

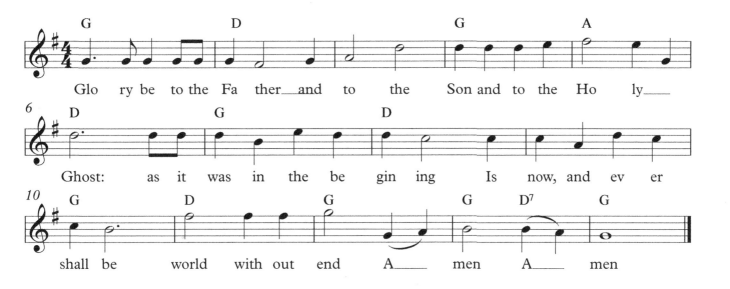

This hymn, also referred to as *The Doxology*, is commonly performed with no additional lyrics.

Go, Tell it on the Mountain

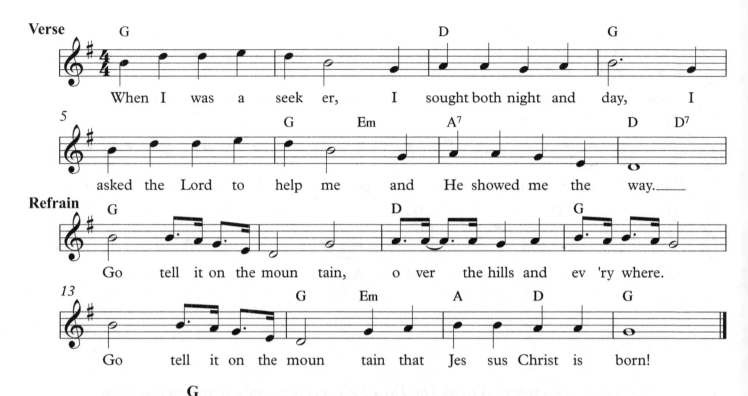

Verse

When I was a seek er, I sought both night and day, I
asked the Lord to help me and He showed me the way.___

Refrain

Go tell it on the moun tain, o ver the hills and ev 'ry where.
Go tell it on the moun tain that Jes sus Christ is born!

G
While shepherds kept their watching
D   **G**
O'er silent flocks by night, **Em**
Behold throughout the heavens
A⁷   **D** **D⁷**
There shown a holy light.
Refrain

G
The shepherds feared and trembled,
D   **G**
When lo! above the earth,
Em
Rang out the angel chorus
A⁷   **D** **D⁷**
That hailed the Savior's birth.
Refrain

G
Down in a lowly manger
D   **G**
The humble Christ was born,
Em
And God sent us salvation
A⁷   **D** **D⁷**
That blessed Christmas morn.
Refrain

68

Holy, Holy, Holy

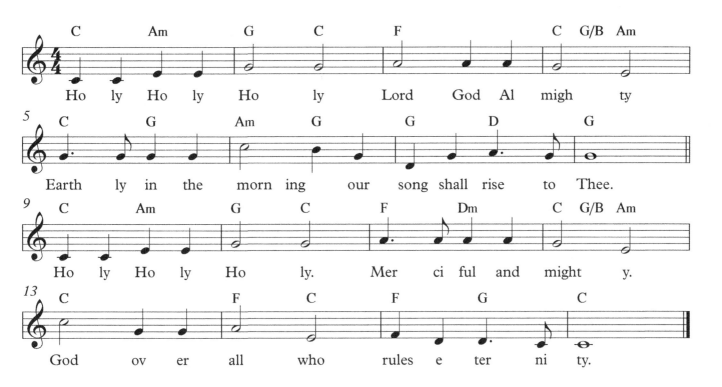

Holy, Holy, Holy, Lord God Almighty
Earthly in the morning our song shall rise to Thee.
Holy, Holy, Holy. Merciful and mighty.
God over all who rules eternity.

Holy, Holy, Holy, All the saints adore Thee
Casting down their golden crowns around the glassy sea
Cherubim and seraphim falling down before Thee
Who was and is and ever more shall be

Holy, Holy, Holy, Through the darkness hide Thee
Through the eye of sinful man Thy glory may not see
Only Thou art holy there is none beside Thee
Perfect in pow'r in love and purity

Holy, Holy, Holy, Lord God Almighty
All thy works shall praise Thy name in earth and sky and sea
Holy, Holy, Holy, merciful and mighty
God in three Persons, blessed Trinity

How Great Thou Art

Verse

O Lord my God, when I in awe some won der con sid er all the worlds Thy hands have

made. I see the stars, I hear the rol ling thunder Thy power through out the un i verse dis

Refrain

played Then sings my soul, my Sav ior God to Thee. How great Thou art how great Thou

art. Then sings my soul, my Sav ior God to Thee. How great Thou art, how great Thou art.

And when I think of God, His Son not sparing,
Sent Him to die, I scarce can take it in
That on the Cross, my burden gladly bearing
He bled and died to take away my sin
Refrain

When Christ shall come with shout of acclamation
And lead me home, what joy shall fill my heart
Then I shall bow with humble adoration
And then proclaim, my God, how great Thou art
Refrain

When through the woods and forest glades I wander
And hear the birds sing sweetly in the trees
When I look down from lofty mountain grandeur
And hear the brook and feel the gentle breeze
Refrain

In The Garden

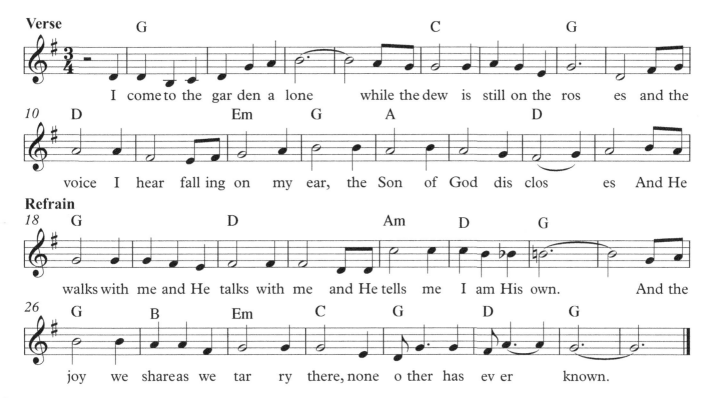

Verse

I come to the gar den a lone while the dew is still on the ros es and the voice I hear fall ing on my ear, the Son of God dis clos es And He

Refrain

walks with me and He talks with me and He tells me I am His own. And the joy we share as we tar ry there, none o ther has ev er known.

He speaks and the sound of His voice
Is so sweet the birds hush their singing,
And the melody that He gave to me
Within my heart is ringing.
Refrain

I'd stay in the garden with Him
Though the night around me be falling,
But He bids me go, thru the voice of woe
His voice to me is calling.
Refrain

Just a Closer Walk With Thee

Through this world of toil and snares, ^C ^{Dm} ^G
If I falter Lord, who cares? ^C
Who with me my burden shares? ^F ^{Dm}
None but Thee, dear Lord, none but Thee. ^C ^G ^{C F C Dm}
Refrain

When my feeble life is o'er, ^C ^{Dm} ^G
Time for me will be no more. ^C
Guide me gently, safely o'er ^F ^{Dm}
To Thy kingdom's shore, to Thy shore. ^C ^G ^{C F C Dm}
Refrain

Leaning on the Everlasting Arms

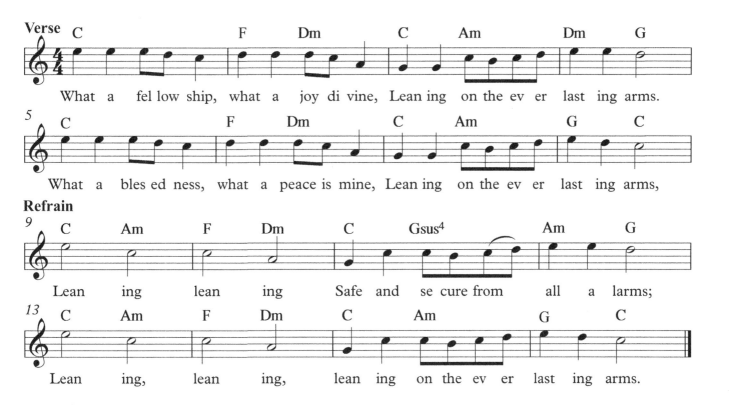

Oh, how sweet to walk in the pilgrim way,
Leaning on the everlasting arms,
Oh, how bright the path grows from day to day,
Leaning on the everlasting arms.

Refrain

What have I to dread, what have I to fear,
Leaning on the everlasting arms?
I have blessed peace with my Lord so near,
Leaning on the everlasting arms.

Refrain

Nearer My God to Thee

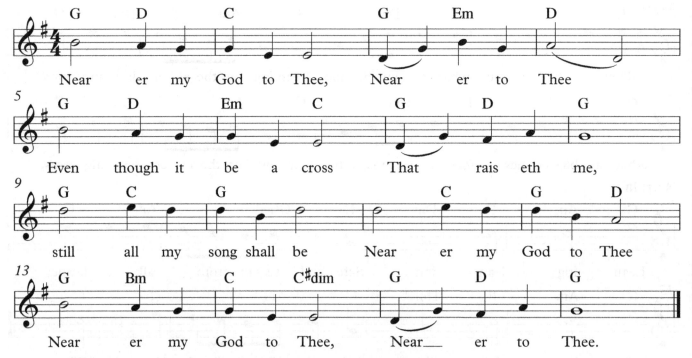

Near er my God to Thee, Near er to Thee

Even though it be a cross That rais eth me,

still all my song shall be Near er my God to Thee

Near er my God to Thee, Near er to Thee.

Though like the wanderer, the sun goes down
Darkness be over me, my rest a stone
Yet in my dreams I'd be nearer my God to Thee
Nearer my God to Thee, Nearer to Thee

There let the way appear, steps unto heav'n
All that Thou sendest me, in mercy given
Angels to beckon me Nearer my God to Thee,
Nearer My God to Thee, Nearer to Thee

Then with my waking thoughts, Bright with Thy praise
Out of my stony griefs, Bethel I'll raise
So by my woes to be Nearer my God to Thee
Nearer my God to Thee, Nearer to Thee

Or if, on joyful wing cleaving the sky
Sun, moon, and stars forgot, upward I fly
Still all my song shall be nearer, my God, to Thee
Nearer, my God, to Thee, nearer to Thee!

Precious Memories

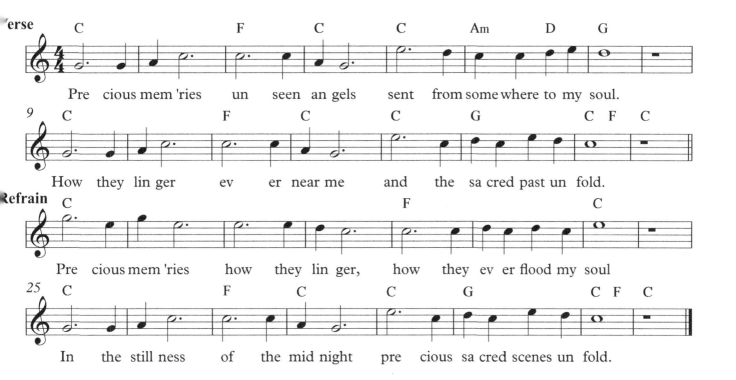

Verse

Pre cious mem 'ries un seen an gels sent from some where to my soul.

How they lin ger ev er near me and the sa cred past un fold.

Refrain

Pre cious mem 'ries how they lin ger, how they ev er flood my soul

In the still ness of the mid night pre cious sa cred scenes un fold.

C   F   C
Precious father, loving mother
C   Am   D   G
Fly across the lonely years
C   F   C
To old home scenes of my childhood
C   G   C   F   C
In fond memory appears

Refrain

C   F   C
In the stillness of the midnight
C   Am   D   G
Echoes of the past I hear
C   F   C
Old-time singing gladness bringing
C   G   C   F   C
From that lovely land somewhere

Refrain

C   F   C
As I travel on life's pathway
C   Am   D   G
I know what life shall hold
C   F   C
As I wander hopes grow fonder,
C   G   C   F   C
Precious mem'ries flood my soul

Refrain

Rock of Ages

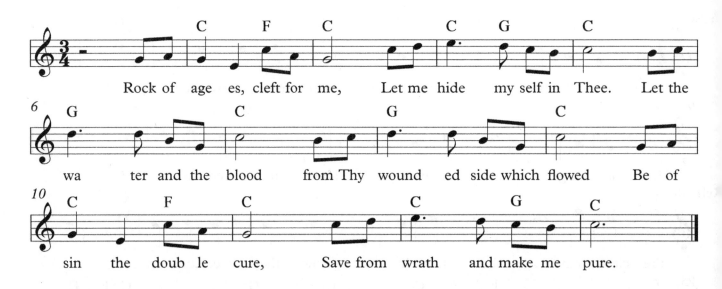

Rock of age es, cleft for me, Let me hide my self in Thee. Let the
wa ter and the blood from Thy wound ed side which flowed Be of
sin the doub le cure, Save from wrath and make me pure.

Not the labors of my hands
Can fulfill Thy law's demands
Could my zeal no respite know
Could my tears forever flow
All for sin could not atone
Thou must save and Thou alone

While I draw the fleeting breath
When my eyes shall close in death.
When I rise to worlds unknown
And behold Thee on Thy throne
Rock of Ages cleft for me
Let me hide myself in Thee

Nothing in my hand I bring,
Simply to the cross I cling
Naked, come to Thee for dress
Helpless, look to Thee for grace
Foul, I to the fountain fly
Wash me, Savior, or I die

Shall We Gather at the River

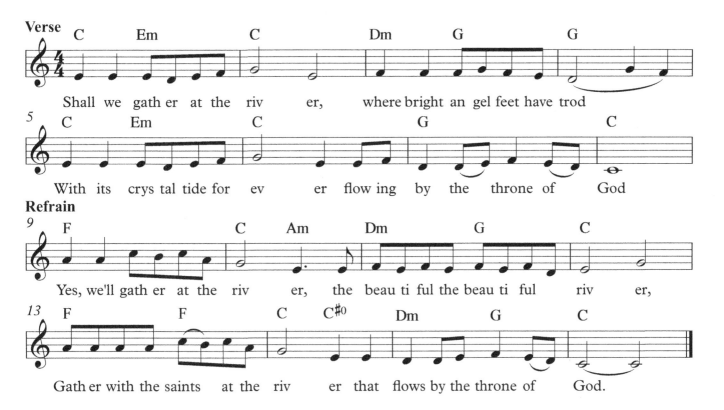

On the margin of the river,
Washing up its silver spray,
We will talk and worship ever,
All the happy golden day.
Refrain

Ere we reach the shining river,
Lay we every burden down,
Grace our spirits will deliver,
And provide a robe and crown.
Refrain

Soon we'll reach the shining river
Soon our pilgrimage will cease,
Soon our happy hearts will quiver
With the melody of peace.
Refrain

Sweet By and By

Verse

There's a land that is fair er than day, and by faith we can see it a far: for the Fa ther waits o ver the way to pre pare us a dwell ing place there. In the

Refrain

sweet by and by, we shall meet on that beau ti ful shore. In the sweet by and by, we shall meet on that beau ti ful shore.

We shall sing on that beautiful shore
The melodious songs of the blessed
And our spirits shall sorrow no more,
Not a sigh for the blessings of rest

Refrain

To our bountiful Father above
We will offer our tribute of praise.
For the glorious gift of His love
And the blessings that hallow our days

Refrain

Swing Low Sweet Chariot

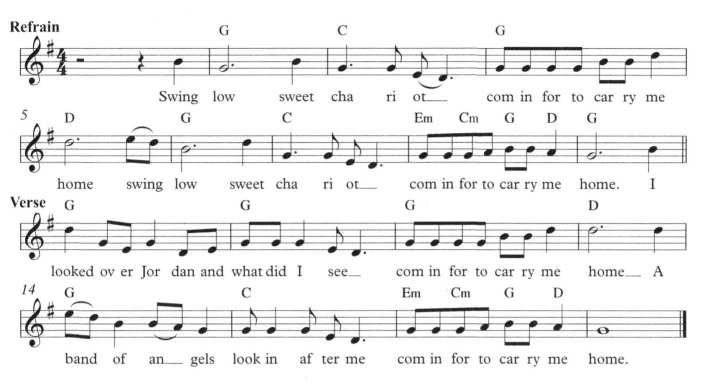

I looked over Jordan and what did I see
Coming for to carry me home
A band of angels coming after me
Coming for to carry me home
Refrain

If you get there before I do
Coming for to carry me home
Tell all my friends I'm coming, too
Coming for to carry me home
Refrain

I'm sometimes up and sometimes down
Coming for to carry me home
But still my soul feels heavenward bound
Coming for to carry me home
Refrain

The Old Rugged Cross

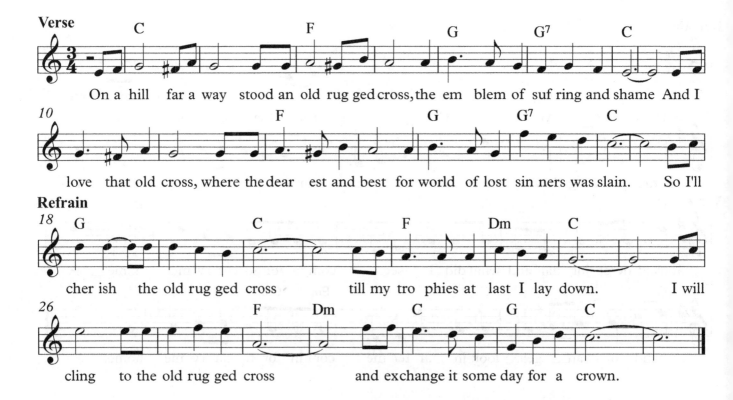

Verse

On a hill far a way stood an old rug ged cross, the em blem of suf ring and shame And I
love that old cross, where the dear est and best for world of lost sin ners was slain. So I'll

Refrain

cher ish the old rug ged cross till my tro phies at last I lay down. I will
cling to the old rug ged cross and exchange it some day for a crown.

O that old rugged cross, so despised by the world,
Has a wondrous attraction for me,
For the dear Lamb of God left His glory above
To bear it to dark Calvary.
Refrain

In that old rugged cross, stained with blood so divine,
A wondrous beauty I see,
For 'twas on that old cross Jesus suffered and died,
To pardon and sanctify me.
Refrain

To that old rugged cross I will ever be true,
Its shame and reproach gladly bear,
Then He'll call me some day to my home far away,
Where His glory forever I'll share.
Refrain

Uncloudy Day

O they tell me of a home where my friends have gone,
O they tell me of a land far away,
Where the tree of life in eternal bloom,
Sheds its fragrance through the uncloudy day
Refrain

O they tell me of a King in His beauty there,
And they tell me that mine eyes shall behold
Where He sits on the throne that is whiter than snow
In the city made of gold
Refrain

What a Friend We Have in Jesus

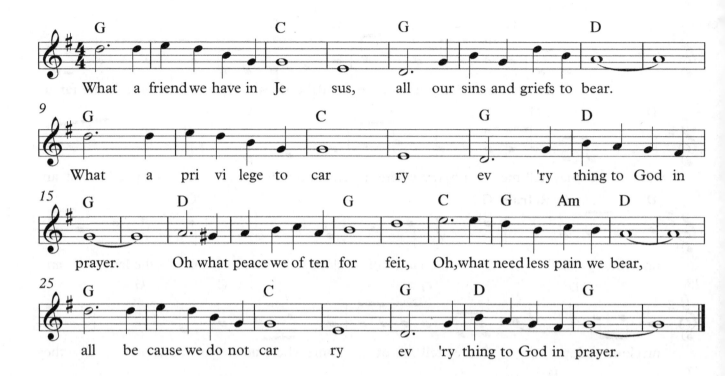

What a friend we have in Je sus, all our sins and griefs to bear.

What a pri vi lege to car ry ev 'ry thing to God in prayer. Oh what peace we of ten for feit, Oh, what need less pain we bear, all be cause we do not car ry ev 'ry thing to God in prayer.

Have we trials and temptations? Is there trouble anywhere?
G   C   G   D

We should never be discouraged, take it to the Lord in prayer.
G   C   G D   G

Can we find a friend so faithful, who will all our sorrows share?
D   G   C   G Am D

Jesus knows our every weakness, take it to the Lord in prayer.
G   C   G D   G

Are we weak and heavy laden, cumbered with a load of care?
G   C   G   D

Precious Savior, still our refuge, take it to the Lord in prayer.
G   C   G D   G

Do thy friends despise, forsake thee? Take it to the Lord in prayer.
D   G   C   G Am D

In His arms He'll take and shield thee, thou will find a solace there.
G   C   G D   G

When the Roll is Called Up Yonder

On that bright & cloudless morning when the dead in Christ shall rise
And the glory of His resurrection share
When His chosen ones shall gather to their home beyond the skies
And the roll is called up yonder I'll be there
Refrain

Let us labor for the Master from the dawn till setting sun
Let us talk of all His wondrous love and care
Then when all of life is over and our work on earth is done
And the roll is called up yonder I'll be there
Refrain

When We All Get to Heaven

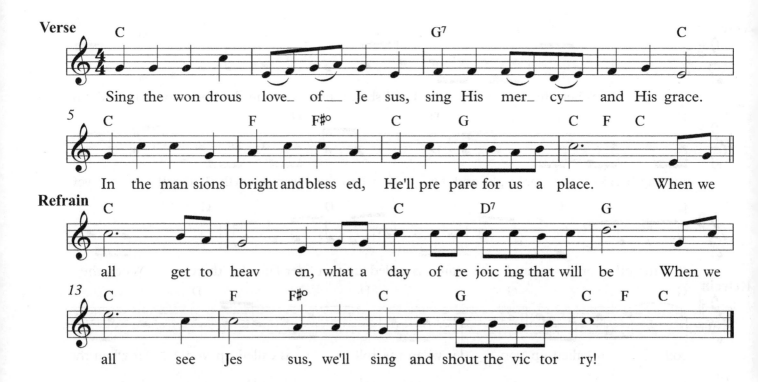

While we walk the pilgrim pathway clouds will overspread the sky
But when trav'ling days are over not a shadow not a sigh
Refrain

Let us then be true and faithful, trusting serving every day
Just one glimpse of Him in glory will the toils of life repay
Refrain

Onward to the prize before us. Soon His beauty we'll behold
Soon the pearly gates will open; We shall tread the streets of gold.
Refrain

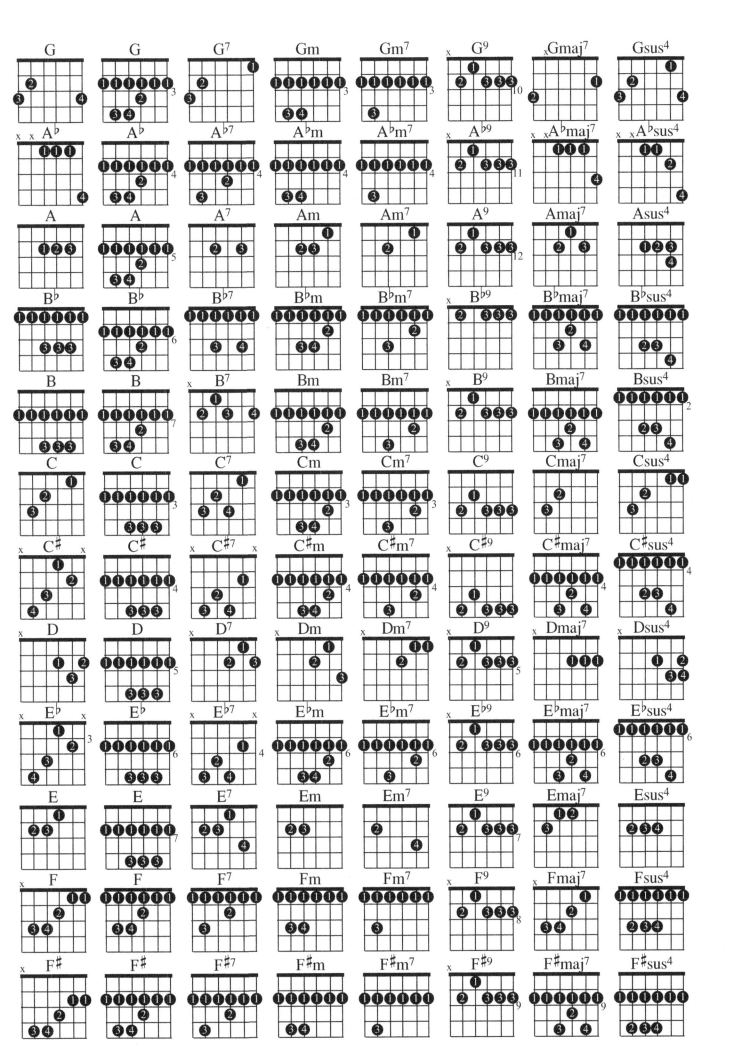

Made in the USA
Las Vegas, NV
18 November 2024

12042172R00050